NEW DAY

GRIEF RECOVERY WORKBOOK

by

Dr. Carolyn M. DeLeon

INKWATER PRESS

PORTLAND • OREGON
INKWATERPRESS.COM

www.inkwaterpress.com

Paperback
ISBN-13 978-1-59299-389-5
ISBN-10 1-59299-389-3

eBook
ISBN-13 978-1-59299-429-8
ISBN-10 1-59299-429-6

Publisher: Inkwater Press

Printed in the U.S.A.
All paper is acid free and meets all ANSI standards for archival quality paper.

3 5 7 9 10 8 6 4 2

Table of Contents

Foreword

As you open this workbook you may be grieving or supporting a loved one or friend through their grief journey. As you embark on this path, it is natural to seek guidance from others who have ventured this road. *New Day: Grief Recovery Workbook* was written for you.

It is within Dr. Carolyn Deleon's first book *Dawning of a New Day* that Carolyn shares her own personal grief journey. With tender simplicity, Carolyn chronicles her own grief journey upon experiencing the tragic and catastrophic suicide death of her husband and life partner. As we venture with Carolyn into unknown territory we witness the shattering realm and intensity of grief's raw emotions. We also begin to witness the gradual unfolding of renewed hope, self-discovery and healing.

It was Carolyn's quest and desire to help others on this path which ultimately led to the *Grief Recovery Workbook*. This is a guide for your journey. Navigate at your own pace, in your own time, as grief often brings confusion and cascades of emotions that surface at any moment in time. Create your own personal time and quiet space to embark upon the workbook. Within its pages you will find suggestions, tips and healing journaling activities.

May you find comfort and support on your journey.

Sally Adelus,
Chief Executive Officer, Hospice of the Valley &
The Community Grief Center, San Jose, California

Introduction

Working through and recovering from grief can be exhausting. Often times you are left wondering where to start and what you can do to help yourself work through your grief. Several good strategies to help the healing process are to work through different activities of self-reflection, and journaling your thoughts, doing various grief recovery activities, and taking care of yourself emotionally, physically and spiritually as well. This workbook is designed to provide varying activities and suggestions that will help you during your grief recovery journey. It is a companion guide to the book *Dawning of a New Day: A Journey Out of Darkness; Life Lessons to Help You Through Grief* by Dr. Carolyn M. De Leon.

Grief is a universal human experience. It is something we all will experience at one time or another in our lives. It is not something we live with continually, it is not something we seek, but it something that we all in the normal course of life will confront. Mel Lawrenz and Daniel Green in their book *Life after Grief* share a definition of grief that says, "Grief is the natural, expected reaction to loss." This is important to understand because it's a *natural part of life* and we should expect to grieve when we have a significant loss of a loved one in our lives. It's not abnormal to grieve or cry as a result of our loss. In fact, grieving and crying hold the powerful keys to unlocking inner healing over time if you allow the process to take place within you.

This workbook is designed to help you self-reflect and write as you walk through your journey of grief and into your new day. Each chapter in the workbook is structured to help you think through and process each phase of your grief. It is also written to help you understand the importance of taking care of yourself, the whole person. This workbook is about *you*. It can be used by individuals or with groups to aid in the healing and recovery process after the loss of a loved one. This workbook is only intended to provide suggestions and ideas for helping you through grief recovery and should not be considered as a substitute for professional therapeutic counseling.

This workbook was compiled from many activities that my own grief counselor from Hospice of the Valley in San Jose, California, suggested that I use, activities and tips that I found helpful during my journey through grief, and others suggestions taken and adapted from many references and resources on grief and bereavement. If you are working alone through this book and not with a group or counselor and you experience overwhelming, uncontrollable emotions, you should stop and seek professional help through your physician, counselor, or therapist.

The journey of grief is unique to every individual. The important part of your healing journey is to try as many things as you can and find what works for you individually. Remember, you will heal over time, the pain won't last forever, but you must allow the grief process to have its way and allow yourself to experience your grief. This is your journey to healing. Peace be with you.

Chapter One

Your First Day

We must accept finite disappointment,
but we must never lose infinite hope.
                    – Martin Luther King, Jr.

Finding out about the death of your loved one, the first day, is shocking and frequently we immediately become numb as we struggle to cope with the news that our loved one has died. Because we are in such a state of shock and numbness we are in a robotic mode and are moving through the motions just to get things done. This chapter begins with suggestions for you to consider during the early phases of your grief. Remember during the early stages of grief from the first day, your thinking and reasoning abilities will be reduced and not functioning at the normal capacity. That's why we need others to help us during this initial stage of grieving.

As you begin your grief journey, here are some recommendations to help during the initial stages of grief

---

- ☙ Establish a support network for yourself.

- ☙ Buy and keep a day planner/calendar to write everything down—your memory will not be at full capacity for quite some time.

- ☙ Have someone help you make and keep appointments.

- ☙ If you have not already had the memorial service, have a trusted friend help you make the arrangements.

- ☙ Allow others to help you during this early time of grief.

- ☙ Allow others to cook meals for you during this time.

- ☙ Try not to make any major life decisions until your emotions have calmed—at least for the first year.

- ☙ Try not to make decisions about your loved one's personal possessions until you are able to think more rationally about what to do with them.

- ☙ Consider getting a grief counselor or therapist to help you work through your grief or consider joining a grief support group in your area.

- ☙ If you have children, get them into counseling as soon as possible to help them find their way of grieving the loss.

If you know someone who has just lost a loved one, these are suggestions for helping grievers

- Provide continual reassurance that they will make it through this time—remind the griever that this time of grief is temporary.

- Initially, grievers will have a difficult time reaching out for help; assign people to call or visit the griever on a regular basis until the griever is comfortable reaching out for help.

- Be prepared to support the griever for at least 1–2 years- if it's a traumatic death often the griever will need more intense support.

- Allow grievers to express their anger toward God and their loved one.

- Be prepared for the extreme emotional outpouring. The griever's emotions will swing back and forth among anger, pain, crying, shock, and frustration. Be accepting.

- Just listening in silence is often what grievers need the most. Someone's presence in silence is often enough to comfort grievers.

- Grievers may want to share their story over and over again—especially a sudden death—listen to their story and don't change the subject.

- Be prepared for questions you cannot answer. Be comfortable saying, "I don't know."

- Encourage grievers, if they were part of a church or religious organization, to participate as often as they are able.

- It's okay to speak of the loved one who died. Often for grievers, it is therapeutic to be able to share things about their loved one.

- Encourage grievers to participate in their grief rituals—things that help them like visiting the cemetery and taking flowers.

Often times we don't get the opportunity to go back and recollect the first day. Recalling the events of the first day, whether sharing the details with someone out loud or writing it down, can help you bring closure to the first day and start down your path to recovery. You may find that you will remember details about the first day that may be helpful to you in healing. Take some time and recall, as you are able to, the events of the first day. Share with your counselor, therapist, friend, or group what your thoughts and memories mean to you.

Describe your first day and what happened when
you discovered your loved one had died:

_____

_____

_____

_____

_____

_____

_____

_____

_____

_____

_____

_____

_____

_____

_____

_____

_____

_____

_____

_____

_____

_____

_____

_____

Did you recall any details of the first day that you had not remembered before? If so, what were they?

_____

_____

_____

_____

_____

How did the details remembered help you?

_____

_____

_____

_____

_____

What emotions did you feel as you were writing? What were they?

_____

_____

_____

_____

_____

Was there any particular event that stood out to you the first day? What was it?

_____

_____

_____

_____

_____

Why do you think this event stood out in your memory?

_____

_____

_____

_____

_____

Describe what your first coping mechanisms were and are you still using those mechanisms? Are they healthy and helpful mechanisms? In what way?

_____

_____

_____

_____

_____

If you happen to be the person who was with your loved one when they died or you found them after they died, and you are experiencing flashbacks of the event, you could be experiencing post-traumatic stress disorder (PTSD) and you should seek professional help immediately. Flashbacks are memories from the past that intrude into your mind in the present and make it seem as though the event is happening right now (Williams and Poijula, 2002). In *The PTSD Workbook*, Williams and Poijula (p. 51) suggest that sometimes when flashbacks occur they are part of the memory of the event that has not been worked through yet and you might ask yourself the following questions:

- What is my flashback telling me?
- Do I have more to feel?
- Do I have more to accept about the death?
- Do I have more to hear?
- Do I have more to see about the event?
- Do I have more to learn about the event?

Suggested Activities for Flashbacks:

The following activities are adapted from Williams and Poijula (2002, p. 51) and they suggest some of these exercises.

Video Tape Activity:

One way to help you control the flashbacks is to place your memories on your own "video tape" in your mind. You have the ability to control playing, fast-forwarding, or rewinding. This technique takes practice to use effectively, and you should try it with a positive memory before you try it with any difficult or traumatic memory that you may be experiencing.

Positive Memory:

The positive event that I am going to practice with is:

_____

_____

_____

_____

_____

When you fast-forward the event what sensory experiences did you have? (e.g., feel, smell, see, and hear)

_____

_____

_____

_____

_____

When you rewind the event, what did you experience?

_____

_____

_____

_____

_____

Grief Event Memory:

The event that I am going to use is:

_____

_____

_____

_____

_____

When you fast-forward the event what sensory experiences did you have? (e.g., feel, smell, see, and hear)

_____

_____

_____

_____

_____

When you rewind the event, what did you experience?

_____

_____

_____

_____

_____

How was this technique helpful for you and did you feel more in control of your memories? Was it easier to use with your positive memory?

_____

_____

_____

_____

_____

Other Techniques (Williams & Poijula, 2002, pp. 55-56):

Listed below are other techniques to handle your flashbacks in the moment they occur and to help you immediately. Not all of them will work, but try them and see what works for you. Remember, if you are not working with a professional counselor or therapist and you continue to experience these flashbacks you should seek professional help in dealing with your flashbacks.

- Repeatedly blink your eyes hard

- Change the position of your body

- Use deep breathing exercises

- Use imagery to go to a safe place in your mind

- Go to your actual safe place

- Hold on to a safe object

- Draw the flashback on paper and physically place in a container or box and then close the container or box until a more appropriate time

- Wash your face with cold water

- In your safe place use art materials—crayons, paints, etc.—to express your emotions or represent your memory

- Get involved in a physical activity such as walking

Chapter Two

Your Story

A loving heart is the truest wisdom.

– Charles Dickens

We all have a story to tell. Telling the story of your loved one or the loss of your loved one is a good way to help you gain a sense of closure with the loss. Particularly if the loss was sudden and unexpected such as suicide or a tragic accident—many individuals find it healing to tell their story over and over again. This will give you an opportunity to write down your story as you experienced it and reread it aloud as you sense the need to recount your story. It is normal to want to repeat your story to people over and over. If you are part of a grief recovery group and you want to share your story with the group, but need something to read, this will be the ideal way to write it down and read it aloud to share with others.

Journal Activity:

Tell your story about your loved one.

Describe who your loved one was and what their life was about.

_____

_____

_____

_____

_____

_____

_____

_____

_____

_____

_____

_____

_____

_____

_____

_____

_____

_____

_____

_____

_____

_____

_____

_____

_____

_____

_____

_____

_____

_____

_____

_____

_____

_____

_____

_____

_____

_____

_____

_____

_____

_____

_____

_____

What do you want to share with others about your loved one?

_____

_____

_____

_____

_____

_____

_____

_____

_____

What will you miss the most about not having your loved one with you?

_____

_____

_____

_____

_____

_____

_____

_____

_____

What will you remember the most about your loved one?

_____

_____

_____

_____

_____

_____

_____

_____

What was the most exciting and fun time you had with your loved one?

_____

_____

_____

_____

_____

_____

_____

_____

_____

_____

If you could say one more thing to your loved one, what would it be?

_____

_____

_____

_____

_____

_____

_____

_____

If you could hear your loved one say one more thing to you, what would it be?

_____

_____

_____

_____

_____

_____

_____

_____

What stories have you heard others tell about your loved one?

_____

_____

_____

_____

_____

_____

_____

_____

_____

_____

Adjective Activity:

Write some specific adjective words or phrases that you have heard others use to describe your loved one: For example, loving, hard-working, and liked to laugh, etc....

  ❧ _____

  ❧ _____

  ❧ _____

  ❧ _____

  ❧ _____

  ❧ _____

  ❧ _____

  ❧ _____

  ❧ _____

  ❧ _____

Write these words and phrases down when you hear them
and put them in a memory book of your loved one.

You have the opportunity to tell your loved one's story and honor them on an on-going basis by contributing to an organization in the name of your loved one. You can donate time or money to the organization of your choice or an organization that your loved one liked. List the organizations that you can consider:

Organizations that I will donate time or
money in honor of my loved one:

🙠 _____

🙠 _____

🙠 _____

🙠 _____

🙠 _____

🙠 _____

🙠 _____

🙠 _____

🙠 _____

🙠 _____

I expect to pass through life but once.
If, therefore, there be any kindness I can show,
or any good thing I can do to any fellow being,
let me do it now,
for I shall not pass this way again.

– William Penn

Chapter Three

Mourning

If suffering went out of life,
courage, tenderness, pity, faith, patience and love
in its divinity would go out of life too.

– Father Andrew, SDC

Mourning is the outward appearance of what is happening within you. You will experience and express mourning differently than anyone else. Your mourning is as unique as your personality and it will change over time. You want to allow yourself to experience the different emotions that you are confronting. Confronting and experiencing the emotions will help you move through your mourning and complete your healing process. Mel Lawrenz and Daniel Green in their book *Life After Grief* write that when we are faced with such overwhelmingly powerful feelings of grief, discouragement, and mourning we often wonder if we are going to make it through and if we will be able to move on. The good news is that we are created in a way that we have powerful internal abilities to survive and renew our emotions.

Journal Activity:

Describe what your time of mourning feels like to you.

_____

_____

_____

_____

_____

Describe what your mourning may look like to others around you.

_____

_____

_____

_____

_____

Describe how you are allowing yourself to mourn the loss of your loved one.

_____

_____

_____

_____

_____

_____

_____

_____

Do you sometimes feel that everyone else has gone back to their "normal" lives and you are stuck? Describe that feeling.

_____

_____

_____

_____

_____

_____

_____

_____

Do you feel like you are resisting the mourning process? Write down some things that you might be able to do to help you release and experience your mourning.

_____

_____

_____

_____

_____

_____

_____

_____

_____

_____

Write down things that you will do like finding a safe place to experience your emotions.

_____

_____

_____

_____

_____

_____

_____

_____

_____

_____

Write down the ways or techniques that you have used to allow yourself to experience your mourning. Were some of those techniques more helpful than others? Continue to use those techniques that are helpful to you and experiment with other ways of helping you to experience your mourning that are meaningful to you.

_____

_____

_____

_____

_____

_____

_____

_____

The purpose of mourning is to heal from your loss. Elisabeth Kübler-Ross (2005) has defined five different phases that most people experience when moving through the anticipatory grief process: Denial, Anger, Bargaining, Depression, and Acceptance. The phases are not experienced in any given order but oftentimes people go back and forth, in and out, of each of the phases. Read the following different grief emotions and check the ones that you have experienced.

- ☐ Shock
- ☐ Numbness
- ☐ Anger
- ☐ Depression
- ☐ Guilt
- ☐ Acceptance
- ☐ Denial
- ☐ Bargaining

Describe how you have confronted each of those phases as you experienced them.

_____

_____

_____

_____

_____

_____

_____

_____

_____

_____

_____

_____

_____

_____

_____

_____

Tips for moving through mourning:

- Remember the emotions of mourning will come and go and are rarely experienced in a defined order.

- Give yourself permission to grieve.

- Find a safe place to experience the emotions of your mourning.

- You can remind others that it is okay to talk of your loved one.

- Remember that others may become overwhelmed at you telling the story repeatedly; it is important to see a counselor who is trained to listen and respond to your mourning.

- Your mourning will be on a different timetable and experienced differently than anyone else.

- Remember, mourning is the outward expression of grief. Constantly ask yourself if you have given yourself permission to mourn your grief.

Wolfelt (2001, pp. 3-8) in his book *Healing Your Grieving Heart* shares that mourning individuals should understand the six needs of mourning:

1. **Acknowledge the reality of the death:** You will first need to understand the loss in your mind and you will gradually acknowledge the loss in your heart.

2. **Embrace the pain of the loss:** This requires you to embrace pain, something that is unnatural to you, but necessary for you to heal.

3. **Remember the person who died:** Keeping your memories alive will help give you hope for your future and help you to heal.

4. **Develop a new self-identity:** You will need to reconstruct your self-identity as your "old" identity is no longer alive. This takes time and effort, but allow yourself to find out who you are.

5. **Search for meaning:** Simply write down all of your "why" questions and explore them with your counselor. You may or may not find answers, but sometimes exploring the why can help bring closure. You need to come to the place of not knowing "why" and releasing it if there are simply no answers to be found. If you cannot find out why, search for how your loved one's death can bring new meaning into your life and your new identity.

6. **Receive ongoing support from others:** We need others to help us through this time of mourning. Allow others to help you, call you, bring you dinner and any other things they may offer. Remember mourning is a process, not a one-time event, and you need others to love you and help you along the journey. ***Tell others how they can help you.***

Write down ways that others can help you: For example, preparing meals or making appointments, etc....

_____

_____

_____

_____

_____

_____

_____

_____

_____

_____

Contact List:

Write down a list of your closest friends or family whom you can contact if you need help in a moment's notice:

I can contact_____,

    their telephone number is: _____

I can contact_____,

    their telephone number is: _____

I can contact_____,

    their telephone number is: _____

I can contact_____,

    their telephone number is: _____

My counselor or therapist emergency contact number:_____

_____

My local pastor or clergy emergency contact telephone number:_____

_____

Grief Loss History

Several grief and bereavement experts such as Kübler-Ross and Kessler (2005), James and Friedman (1998), and Jeffreys (2005) suggest that grievers write down a grief loss history graph. As a griever you should be aware of the number of losses that you have experienced over the years. Remember that if you have unresolved grief in your life from a previous loss, you are likely to experience grief from your prior loss as well. Include all loss including the current death of your loved one, death of a family member, pets, close friends, divorce, jobs, etc.…

Plot your grief loss history in the following graph:

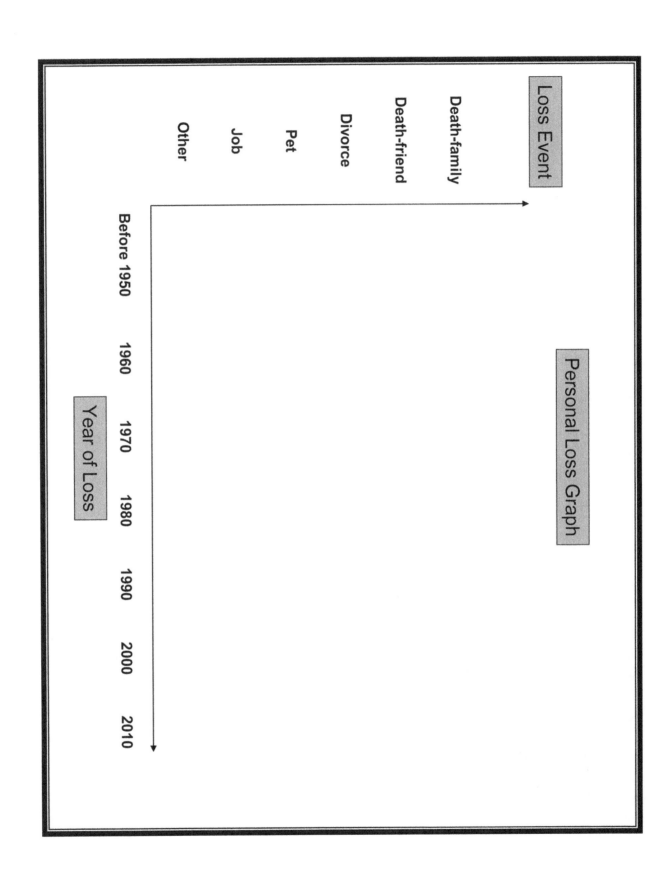

Looking at your loss graph, what do you observe about your history?

_____

_____

_____

_____

_____

Do you think or feel that you have any unresolved grief from a previous loss? Explain why.

_____

_____

_____

_____

_____

Did reviewing your loss history trigger any emotions for you? What were they?

_____

_____

_____

_____

_____

What have you learned about life and loss over your lifetime?

_____

_____

_____

_____

_____

Should you shield the canyons from the windstorms you would
never see the true beauty of their carvings.
— Elizabeth Kubler-Ross

Chapter Four

Guilt and Depression

There is a land of the living and
a land of the dead, and the bridge is love.

– Thornton Wilder

Guilt and depression are symptoms that accompany the grief process. Frequently with a sudden death or a death by suicide, guilt is the emotion that is the most difficult to overcome. Guilt and depression are normal emotions that grieving individuals experience—especially if the death is from suicide. When walking through grief and experiencing guilt and depression, it is a good strategy to get professional counseling and have a professional help you through these very serious and difficult stages of grief. John Hewett in his book *After Suicide* shares that the most serious feelings of guilt come after a spouse's suicide and the feelings of guilt that arise can be: What did I do to cause this? Could I have prevented it? Guilt is the defining emotion that often separates suicide survivor's grief from non-suicide survivor's grief.

Do you ever have times of feeling "If only I had"...or "I should have..."? Write about these times:

_____

_____

_____

_____

_____

Often times when you get the "If only..." thoughts, stop and remember that there is nothing you could have done to prevent the death and those thoughts are the brain's way of trying to make sense of the death and figure out how you could have changed the events, even though you couldn't.

Describe your thoughts about feeling responsible for your loved one's death. Share your thoughts with your counselor, therapist, or trusted friend who can help you look beyond these feelings.

_____

_____

_____

_____

_____

Ginsburg (2004) writes that guilt is the greatest avoidance tool that we have. If you look at the other side of guilt it's really fear or anger that's residing within you. You may be feeling guilty that you were not the one who died, or you did not make your loved one go to the doctor sooner, or that you could have prevented your loved one's death if only you had done something different, or you may feel guilty that a long illness is over. Sometimes I refer to that feeling as bitter-sweet. The bitterness comes from the loss; the sweet part is your loved one is no longer suffering.

Remember there will always be things that we could have done differently, but we do the best we can in the moment with the knowledge that we have. That old cliché is true, we have 20/20 hindsight. But in the moment, you have done what you are capable of doing. If you are experiencing guilty feelings as part of your grief process, you must overcome your feelings of guilt if you are going to move completely through your grief process. Read the following statements and questions, self-reflect about your feelings of guilt, and write down your thoughts.

There isn't anything you could have done to prevent the death.

_____

_____

_____

_____

_____

Do you think your loved one blames you? Why?

_____

_____

_____

_____

_____

What do you think your loved one would say to you now?

_____

_____

_____

_____

_____

Stop beating yourself up and saying to yourself, "I should have…" What thoughts do you continually have that you need to stop beating yourself up with? Write them down.

_____

_____

_____

_____

_____

Tell yourself out loud to stop when you know you are having thoughts of guilt. Talk to yourself and visualize yourself telling your loved one that you did the best you could. Write down how you feel after seeing yourself tell your loved one.

_____

_____

_____

_____

_____

In *Life after Grief*, Lawrenz and Green (1995, p. 91) say the following symptoms are serious signs of depression and if you are experiencing these symptoms, you should seek professional psychological or therapeutic help for your depression.

- Physical disturbances—weight loss or gain, loss of appetite, increase in appetite or insomnia
- A sense of despair or hopelessness about life
- A sense of personal worthlessness, shame, or no self-esteem
- Inability to function in your normal environment (at home, at work)—crying excessively or pervasive sadness
- Suicide thoughts
- When these signs occur after a significant amount of time has passed from the loss
- When these signs become a regular pattern after several months
- Isolating and withdrawing from others

Write or talk with a friend, therapist or counselor about any feelings you are having from the above list of normal feelings of grief, especially if the feelings are lasting for more than several weeks.

_____

_____

_____

_____

_____

_____

_____

_____

_____

Sadness is a normal part of the grief process. Sadness related to the loss and the grief process can turn into depression. If you have been experiencing ongoing depression it should be addressed with a professional counselor or licensed psychologist or therapist.

List the things that help boost your mood such as sitting in the sun, walking or exercising, or listening to music. Try to incorporate each of these things into your daily routine or several days of the week.

1. _____

2. _____

3. _____

4. _____

5. _____

6. _____

7. _____

8. _____

Use the Model below to color shade how you are feeling each day of the week. Use black if you're feeling depressed, use blue if you feel at peace, use different colors to represent how you are feeling. This will give you a visual track record that you can monitor yourself that has meaning to you. Write down the meaning that each of the colors has to you:

1. Red_____

2. Orange_____

3. Yellow_____

4. Green_____

5. Blue_____

6. Purple_____

7. Black_____

8. Pink_____

9. White_____

10. Others_____

Write down if any of the activities above make a difference in your daily moods and feelings. Copy this page and use it on a weekly basis.

Each morning, afternoon and evening, color the octagons to represent how you are feeling at that time of day. Try to observe if there are certain times of day when you feel more emotional than other times.

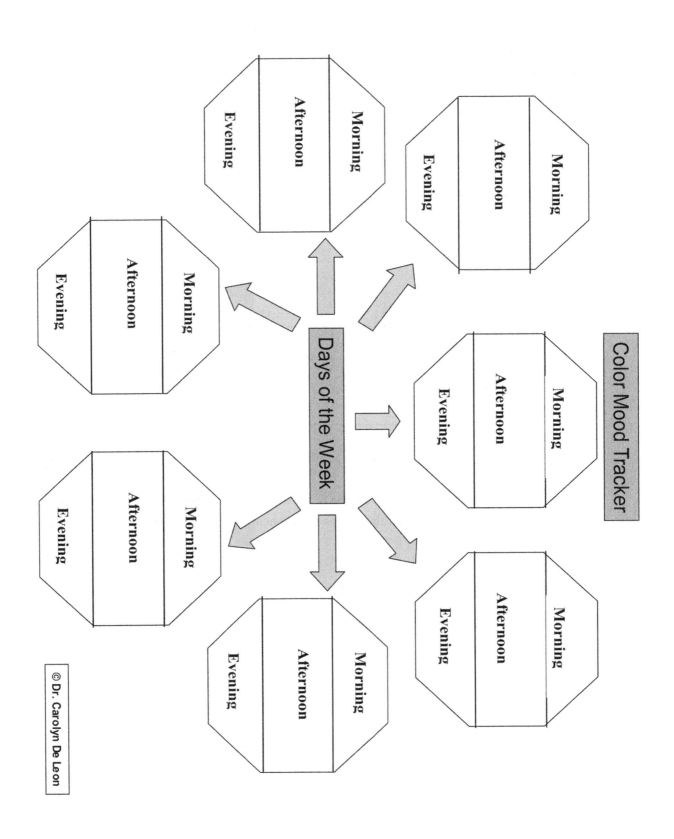

Chapter Five

Anger and Pain

Forgiveness is an act of the will
and the will can function regardless
of the temperature of the heart.

– Corrie ten Boom

Anger and pain are a normal part of the grieving process and they are emotions that you will experience. The key to moving through the stages of anger and pain is experiencing them and letting out the anger and pain in a healthy way. You will need to find healthy strategies to release your anger and pain that won't harm you or anyone else. The anger and feelings of pain can rise up within you at any moment. Give yourself the space to deal with the emotion at the moment it rises if at all possible. Elisabeth Kübler-Ross and David Kessler in their book *On grief and Grieving* share that anger does not need to be logical and anger usually arises once you've reached a state of feeling safe and knowing that you are going to make it through this time of loss. Anger usually means that you are moving through the grief process. Be aware of your anger and let it out in a healthy way so that it will not be harmful to others. If you're having difficulty controlling your anger, seek professional help.

Activity:

> **Sometimes the feeling of anger can overcome us and can cause us to feel overwhelming guilt, but it has the potential to keep us locked up inside. Describe your feelings of "This is not fair," "Why is this happening to me," or even feeling anger toward your loved one's death for causing all of your pain.**

_____

_____

_____

_____

_____

_____

_____

_____

_____

_____

Frequently you feel physical pain in some part of your body as a result of grieving. Try to identify where your "pain" hurts in your body (chest, neck, headaches, heart, etc.).

_____

_____

_____

_____

_____

Anger is a normal part of living through a traumatic death (loss). Below are some ways to release our angry feelings. The following strategies were helpful recommendations from my counselor, a licensed clinical social worker, to deal with anger.

- ℞ Punch a pillow

- ℞ Scream (away from others where you feel safe)

- ℞ Write or journal your feelings of anger

- ℞ Talk and talk, cry as much as you can (be sure to be with someone you trust who will listen and be non-judgmental)

- ℞ Sometimes when you have a difficult time getting your tears out it can help to listen to music or even watch a movie that you know will bring your emotions to the surface and release your tears

- ℞ When you feel anger and pain welling up inside, get a piece of white paper and scribble on it with a black crayon. This will help give you a visual of the anger and pain as you are releasing it.

Write down if any of the strategies above have helped you. If you have found other strategies, write below what those strategies are.

- ℞ _____

- ℞ _____

- ℞ _____

- ℞ _____

- ℞ _____

- ℞ _____

- ℞ _____

- ℞ _____

- ℞ _____

- ℞ _____

You can help yourself to confront and dissipate the anger and pain by using relaxation and calming exercises. You can use visualization strategies or listen to calming relaxation music. Read the following strategies and check the ones you have used and write how they have helped you.

- ☐ Visualize yourself in your most peaceful place
- ☐ Listen to relaxation music such as ocean sounds
- ☐ Lie outside in the shade, on the grass, and gaze into the sky
- ☐ Deep breathing exercises
- ☐ Go for a walk in the mountains, on the beach or in a park
- ☐ Take a walk in the rain
- ☐ Get a massage
- ☐ Get a pedicure, manicure, or both
- ☐ Take a hot bubble bath
- ☐ Pamper yourself
- ☐ Other (write your strategies down)

_____

_____

_____

_____

Frequently when you experience anger in your grief process there may be a need to forgive your loved one for dying. When you have unforgiveness, it has the potential to keep you locked in a state of anger and bitterness. Forgiveness is possible and you can be released from your anger by forgiving your loved one. Sometimes you don't realize that you have unforgiveness in your heart; take some time to reflect and release forgiveness toward your loved one, toward yourself, toward another family member, or sometimes people feel the need to forgive God.

Sometimes our life circumstances with the loved one who has died make us feel like we can't forgive them because they hurt us when they were alive. Remember that being able to forgive someone who has hurt you is a process and it doesn't happen overnight. Give yourself permission to think about it. If you are experiencing overwhelming anger and hurt because of your loved one, I suggest you work with a therapist or counselor who can help you work through the sensitive issues.

Take some time to read and think about the following statements and write down the first thing comes to your mind.

      ❧ I blame_____for _____

      ❧ I blame_____for_____

      ❧ I'm angry with_____for_____

      ❧ I'm angry with_____for_____

Now take some time and write then say aloud that you forgive whoever has hurt you. You may have to repeat this aloud daily until you feel the release. Forgiveness is a choice—your choice.

      ❧ I forgive_____for_____

      ❧ I forgive_____for_____

      ❧ I forgive_____for_____

      ❧ I forgive_____for_____

Chapter Six

Faith and Grief

The struggle to believe is possibly the mightiest conflict known to the soul of man. Faith does not always come from quiet contemplation or meditation. It is sometimes born among the raging questions with no answers, pain with no relief, hope that has no reason to exist.

– Glenn Owen, Foreword
The Gift of Life, By Randy Becton

Frequently after the loss of a loved one, particularly a sudden loss, our spiritual faith may seem as though it has been shattered. This chapter is written from a Judeo-Christian faith perspective. You may or may not have any faith or a religious affiliation. If you don't have a Christian religious affiliation or you have a religion other than Christianity, you may want to skip over this chapter. Whatever your religious affiliation, you still may find some of the activities and advice helpful for you during your grief recovery journey.

Many people feel and you may feel like God has abandoned you and that you are facing the challenge of your loss alone without God. We have been created to grieve in response to loss. Because of the magnitude of our emotions we are often unable to sense our spiritual side and thus it can leave you with the feeling that God has left you. Be assured that the one who will never leave you during your most intense hour of need—is God. There are times during your grief recovery when you will face challenges having faith and believing. That is normal. During those times you should verbalize and ask God the tough questions. God created you to grieve and He wants you to come to Him and ask your questions. Answers may come quickly or answers may come slowly or not at all. During this time you are truly walking by faith.

Do not abandon your faith or religion, but give yourself time to walk through the grieving process. You will eventually recover over time and be able to participate in spiritual exercises.

As you walk through your journey, remember you still have faith in you, it's only temporarily difficult to access. Eventually, when you come through to the other side of grief you will be able to help someone else walk the same road you are walking now. St. Paul in 2 Corinthians talks about the comfort that we receive from others being the same comfort we will give to others when they walk through similar circumstances. There is grace and hope available for you during this difficult time.

Writing a prayer to God can also be helpful to express your thoughts to God. Take some time and write your own prayer—don't hold anything back. Write out whatever emotions and thoughts you want to express to God.

_____

_____

_____

_____

_____

_____

_____

_____

_____

Faith is actually your belief. Lawrenz and Green (1995b) share that it is important to hold on to something that is greater than yourself during times of loss. Most people find it difficult to worship or to participate in a spiritual service because of the raw emotions of grief. As you feel you are able to engage in spiritual disciplines, take them one at a time as you begin to rebuild your spiritual life.

Meditation Activity:

It can be helpful to meditate on different quotes. Read the following verses and quotes and meditate upon them. Write down whatever comes to you—whether positive or negative.

"Blessed are those who mourn, for they will be comforted." (Matthew 5:4) NIV

_____

_____

_____

_____

_____

"A smile is the beginning of peace"
– Mother Teresa

_____

_____

_____

_____

_____

"Even though I walk though the dark valley of death, because you are with me, I fear no harm. Your rod and your staff give me courage." (Psalm 23:4) NAS

_____

_____

_____

_____

_____

"I have held many things in my hands, and I have lost them all; but whatever I have placed in God's hands, that I still possess."
–Martin Luther

_____

_____

_____

_____

_____

"There is a time for everything, and a season for every activity under heaven: a time to be born and a time to die, a time to plant and a time to uproot, a time to kill and a time to heal, a time to tear down and a time to build up, a time to weep and a time to laugh, a time to mourn and a time to dance, a time to scatter stones and a time to gather them, a time to embrace and a time to refrain, a time to search and a time to give up, a time to keep and a time to throw away, a time to tear and a time to mend, a time to be silent and a time to speak, a time to love and a time to hate, a time for war and a time for peace." (Ecclesiastes 3:1-8) NIV

_____

_____

_____

_____

_____

"You never find yourself until you face the truth"
– Pearl Bailey

_____

_____

_____

_____

_____

"You cannot always control what goes on outside, but you can always control what goes on inside."
– Anonymous

_____

_____

_____

_____

_____

Listening to relaxation, instrumental or worship music is a good strategy to calm your soul and spirit. It helps to move your thoughts away from your grief for a short time and direct your thoughts toward peaceful places and ideas. Take some time to dim the lights, sit down in a comfortable place, and close your eyes and simply listen to the music or the words of the songs. Allow yourself to visualize beautiful places, and think positive thoughts.

Write down how you are feeling after you engage in this activity:

_____

_____

_____

_____

_____

Reflect and write down how you think your faith has changed or is changing as a result of the death of your loved one and walking through grief.

_____

_____

_____

_____

_____

Strategies for rebuilding your faith:

- ☙ Realize that you are different and your relationship with God is now different.

- ☙ Find new ways of communing with God. Instead of only praying, take a walk in a park, in the mountains, on a beach, or just outside in an area of nature to feel closer to God.

- ☙ Be aware of new ways that God may be speaking to you or leading you in life.

- ☙ Continue to participate in your worship services even if you can only participate for short time at the beginning.

- ☙ Keep your relationships with people who have a similar faith.

Think about your faith and write down some things about your faith that have changed or are different: Do you consider these things positive or negative?

- ☙ _____

- ☙ _____

- ☙ _____

- ☙ _____

- ☙ _____

From what you have learned about your faith during your grief journey—how might you be able to help someone else traveling the same road?

_____

_____

_____

_____

_____

Bob Deits (2000, pp.120-123) in his book *Life After Loss* shares four distinct ways that holding on to your faith can help you after the loss of a loved one:

1. Your faith can influence your fundamental view of life.
2. Your faith can provide the motivation you need for grief recovery.
3. Your faith is a great antidote for the loneliness that accompanies every loss.
4. Your faith community or church group can provide supportive strength.

Don't give up your faith, but lean into your faith to help you walk through life's most challenging times—the loss of a loved one. During the difficult seasons of faith is when the roots of your faith will grow deeper and you will come out stronger on the other side of grief.

The ideals that have lighted my way and, time after time,
have given me new courage to face life cheerfully
have been Kindness, Beauty, and Truth.
– Albert Einstein

Chapter Seven

Grieving Rituals and New Traditions

Believe that life is worth living,
And your belief will help create the fact.

— William James

Grieving rituals, whether you continue them or not, can help you in the journey of grief to bring healing and closure to the death of your loved one. Some of the annual rituals that I participated in that were the most helpful to me, but I no longer need, were 1) Placing an ornament in memory of my husband on the Hospice of the Valley Christmas Tree lighting downtown, 2) Having my husband prayed for in annual Catholic prayer mass, 3) Taking flowers to the grave on special occasions. It's okay to have grieving rituals to help you soften the pain of your loss and it's also okay to start new traditions.

Your new traditions will become part of your new life and your new day as you move on with your life. It's okay to start new traditions for yourself or your family. You will need new traditions because you are redefining your new life with new routines.

Describe a ritual that has helped you feel some comfort after the loss of your loved one.

_____

_____

_____

_____

_____

Do those close to you support you or join you during the grieving rituals that are precious and valuable to you?

_____

_____

_____

_____

_____

Sometimes when you create or participate in new grieving rituals, you may feel you're being judged or criticized by others as you move through your grieving process (e.g., keeping your loved one's belongings, the way you need your time alone, going to the cemetery, etc.) .

Write down or talk about how you perceive others are seeing your grieving rituals. How can you, in a healthy way, explain to others what these rituals mean to you?

_____

_____

_____

_____

_____

_____

_____

_____

_____

Talk (write) about people in your life who support you and allow you to be who you are in this growing process.

_____

_____

_____

_____

_____

_____

_____

_____

_____

What new traditions have you begun since the loss of your loved one? Have you begun new traditions for holidays or special occasions?

_____

_____

_____

_____

_____

_____

_____

_____

_____

_____

Special times of the year come to every griever when you will remember the special dates with your loved one. You should have a plan to do something either to remember and celebrate your loved one or to be with close friends during those times.

Write down what you will do and who you will be with during these special dates:

    ℞ Birthday of your loved one:

        I plan to_____

        I will be with_____

    ℞ Anniversary dates:

        I plan to_____

        I will be with_____

    ℞ Christmas:

        I plan to_____

        I will be with_____

    ℞ Thanksgiving:

        I plan to _____

        I will be with_____

    ❧ Other holidays:

        I plan to_____

        I will be with_____

    ❧ Anniversary of your loved one's death:

        I plan to_____

        I will be with_____

    ❧ Your own birthday:

        I plan to_____

        I will be with_____

New traditions for your new life:

Creating new traditions that are uniquely yours are important in rebuilding your life and moving on from your place of grief. Take some time to reflect about fun things, new things, or things you've always wanted to do, and write down what new traditions you can begin in your new life:

My New Traditions

New holiday tradition: _____

New birthday tradition: _____

New traveling tradition: _____

New reading tradition: _____

New exercise tradition: _____

New outdoor tradition: _____

New religious tradition: _____

New social tradition: _____

New family tradition: _____

Chapter Eight

Memories and Good-Byes

When one door closes another opens.
But we often look so long and so regretfully upon the closed
door that we fail to see the one that has opened for us.
– Alexander Graham Bell

Memories will be one thing that you will always have with you. Your memories are yours and no one can take them away. Your memories can serve to keep your loved one alive in your heart, but memories also have the potential to keep you locked in a state of grief. It is important that you find a way to preserve your memories and say good-bye. Saying good-bye is not easy because it means you are acknowledging that your loved one is truly gone.

Often when we lose someone we love it takes us a long time to actually remember what their life was like and all the things about them that we enjoyed.

Write about your loved one's personality traits that you admired and cared about. Write or talk about some things you did together that made you smile.

_____

_____

_____

_____

_____

_____

_____

_____

_____

_____

The special days such as the person's birthday, anniversary, your child's wedding day—and she/he isn't there to be part of this beautiful event—can bring many emotions to the surface, even years later. This is normal. It's important to let those feelings out as they come up. We can do that in many ways.

Suggestions for remembering your loved one:

- Celebrate your loved one's birthday by going to a special place that you both loved.
- Place a memorial in a local newspaper.
- During holiday time honor your loved one with family and friends.
- During the special memory time be sure and ask people to share a humorous memory about your loved one. Laughter can be very healing.

What are some ways you would like to honor your loved one?

_____

_____

_____

_____

_____

_____

_____

_____

_____

_____

It can help to create a memory book of your loved one. We can ask people who knew her/him well to write a memory or two for our book. Photos can also be healing, but often it takes longer for us to be able to look at photos, so words may be easier at first. Often times if you include some of the crazy and fun times, it can help you release the joyful emotion, which you experienced with your loved one. Laughter is great for your healing process.

Memory Book activity:

- Buy a photo album or scrapbook that can hold photos and other items that are important from your life with your loved one.

- Place postcards, poetry, any written item that someone has given you, or even items written by your loved one.

- Create theme pages that represent who your loved one was.

- Take your time organizing these items, don't rush into it; this is a healing exercise and can take time.

A letter to your loved one activity:

Writing a letter to your loved one can also be a helpful way to get your feelings out. At first it may be difficult to write to your loved one. If that's the case, draft a letter to a good friend who lives far away and cannot come and support you now. Tell your friend all about what happened and how you're feeling. Let your feelings flow.

When you're ready, you can write your letter to your loved one. Describe exactly what you're experiencing since she/he has died. This may sound strange to some because you won't be mailing this letter, but the act of putting your feelings on paper addressed to your loved one can be very helpful. Sometimes

people make a ritual out of the letter-writing exercise, and have a ceremony on a beach somewhere and burn the letter. Other times it can be helpful to keep the letter yourself to look back on later on to see how different you may feel.

Here is a sample letter that I wrote to my husband after his suicide:

December 8, 1996

Dear David,

I'm writing this letter to you because I have a lot of things I need to say to you and because I miss you very much. You see, when you were here, I could sit and talk to you about how I was feeling. You were always good about just listening.

There was something about having my husband always there if I felt like I was struggling. Whether it was sadness, anger, or frustration, you were always there to help me. I always had peace after talking with you. I feel as if I don't have any faith right now. I feel as though everything about me, who I was, has just been stripped off layer by layer, and now I really don't know who this person is that remains. I miss you.

Right now I wish I could just see your face, look into your beautiful green eyes, and tell you that your life truly counted. I want to tell you that you touched others in a powerful way. You always had an ability to reach beyond the circumstances of our lives, your own pain, and to touch others. What happened?

I think about you at the moment you killed yourself. I think about the tremendous amount of pain you must have been in at that moment. The thoughts are like arrows that shoot right through my heart. It's so overwhelming for me when I think about these things that I become paralyzed, frozen, and I don't know what to do.

I'm sorry to say that since you committed suicide, my entire life, the very foundation, has been shaken. My friends have loved me anyway.

I don't know if I'll make it. I so desperately need peace and to be healed of the brokenness inside. When I found you dead in your wheelchair, your eyes just staring through me, your face sickly looking, your body cold and stiff—I lost something within me. It shook me to the very core. I was very scared; I still am. My confidence in life just drained out of me. My confidence in my ability to teach, in my ability at work is now gone. It's been a terrible time trying to regain my confidence that I'm really going to make it.

In this dark night of my soul, in the valley of the shadow of death, it's so hard to see any light. I'm feeling like I can't go on. What is life without hope? Nothing—black, obsolete, I see nothing for the future. I need new hope and joy back into my heart.

I'm so very sorry that we didn't have the opportunity to fulfill all the dreams and visions we held in our hearts. Maybe one day I'll find the ability to dream and hope again. I miss talking to you, I miss you holding me, and I miss seeing your smiling face.

I want you to know that I'm going to grief counseling, because I'm having such a hard time dealing with your suicide. Some days I think I'm going to make it; other days I don't think I'll make it another minute. I often wonder why you didn't leave me a note or anything at all. You hurt me deeply. Do you see me now? Do you see the pain and anguish that just rage through my soul day after day? Do you really think I can go on in life this way?

Store this letter in heaven with you.
Carolyn

Write Your Letter:

_____

_____

_____

_____

_____

_____

_____

_____

_____

_____

_____

_____

_____

_____

_____

_____

_____

_____

_____

_____

_____

_____

_____

_____

_____

_____

_____

_____

_____

Saying Good-bye:

Write down some ways that you have already begun to say good-bye to your loved one:

- Example: I went to the cemetery and verbally said good-bye or I wrote a good-bye letter and saved it.

- _____

- _____

- _____

- _____

- _____

- _____

- _____

- _____

- _____

- _____

List some ways that you are preserving your loved one's memory:

❧ _____

❧ _____

❧ _____

❧ _____

❧ _____

❧ _____

❧ _____

❧ _____

❧ _____

❧ _____

Have you observed others saying good-bye to your loved one? What have you observed?

_____

_____

_____

_____

_____

_____

_____

_____

_____

_____

In what positive ways are others preserving your loved one's memory?

_____

_____

_____

_____

_____

_____

_____

_____

_____

It is not the level of prosperity that
makes for happiness but the kinship
of the heart to heart and the way we look at the world.
Both attitudes are within our power, so that a man is happy so long
as he chooses to be happy, and no one can stop him.
– Aleksandr Solzhenitsyn

Chaper Nine

Suddenly Single

We should never let our fears hold us back
from pursuing our hopes.

– John F. Kennedy

If you have lost your spouse, you now are suddenly single. Officially, you are now referred to as a widow or widower. You never imagined that you would have that title! You may be single and alone or single and raising children. In either situation you now have to live life alone, figure out who you are, and begin rebuilding your new life as a single adult. Once you have begun to come through your grief you will begin to ask yourself, "Who am I?" "What is my life for?" "How do I create my own life?" Becoming suddenly single has the potential for creating an identity crisis. You are transitioning from doing everything in life with a partner, to doing everything in life single. It will be frustrating at first, but stay open to new ways of accomplishing daily tasks and routines as you begin rebuilding the foundation in your life.

Often after we lose our partner, we lose our identity. We were part of a team. We awoke each day next to someone we loved, and now we awaken alone. Do you feel empty or afraid? Write about the role change in your life. It's okay here to let your pain and anger flow.

_____

_____

_____

_____

_____

_____

_____

_____

_____

_____

Identity exercise:

Take some time to write down how you have been identified over the years:

- Example: A wife for 20 years.
- _____
- _____
- _____
- _____
- _____
- _____
- _____
- _____
- _____

Reflect on who you want to become or who you want to be known as. See it in your mind and write down some phrases that describe the person you want to be:

- _____
- _____
- _____
- _____
- _____
- _____
- _____
- _____
- _____
- _____

Do you feel uncomfortable when the couples you used to spend time with invite you to spend time with them and your partner isn't there to share it with? Do you go? Do you isolate? Write or talk about how that feels.

_____

_____

_____

_____

_____

_____

_____

_____

_____

The Suddenly Single Struggles:

Put a check mark next to the things that you are most fearful of or that you most struggle with being suddenly single:

- ☐ Sleeping alone
- ☐ Waking up alone
- ☐ Raising children by yourself
- ☐ Going home to an empty house
- ☐ Taking care of the finances
- ☐ Doing all of the household chores
- ☐ Eating alone
- ☐ Socializing
- ☐ Beginning to date
- ☐ Creating your own identity
- ☐ Setting new personal goals
- ☐ Setting new professional goals

Below are some strategies that you can use to help yourself overcome the fears and struggles of the items you may have checked above:

☐ Sleeping and waking up alone: Use a long pillow next to you so that you feel something next to you when you sleep. When you awaken—open up the shades and let sunlight into your room to remind you it's a new day. Say aloud, "Thank you for a new day!"

☐ Make sure that your children have a grief counselor so they can grieve in their own way. Ask family and friends who can be role models for your children to help you with them.

☐ For financial matters, seek out a good financial advisor at the recommendation of friends.

☐ If you do not have children, consider getting a pet. When you come home alone, turn on some instrumental music and create a relaxing environment. Take time to call a friend. Take time to do some personal reading. Take time to care for yourself during this season.

☐ Develop a new routine to do weekly household chores. Get children involved if you have them and they are old enough. As necessary, if you don't want to fix things yourself, hire a handyman to make repairs around the house.

☐ Continue to set your dinner place at the table. If you have children, dine with them. When going out to eat alone, take along something to read.

☐ Continue to go out with friends and go to new places for socializing. Be open to meeting new people. Sometimes you'll have to make yourself socialize as it can be easier to stay home on your couch.

☐ You'll know when you're ready to date. Take your time and simply get to know others that you are dating. Be aware of rebound and not getting involved and remarried too quickly. Allow yourself to learn what dating is about all over again.

☐ Write some things that you can do to begin creating your new identity. For example, opening your own checking account, getting a new hairstyle, or joining a gym.

 ☞ _____

 ☞ _____

 ☞ _____

 ☞ _____

 ☞ _____

☐ Write down some personal and professional goals that you have not ever had time to accomplish, but you have always wanted to do:

    ❧ _____

    ❧ _____

    ❧ _____

    ❧ _____

    ❧ _____

☐ What steps can you take to begin to accomplish some of these goals?

    ❧ _____

    ❧ _____

    ❧ _____

    ❧ _____

    ❧ _____

☐ When will you begin to do these steps? Write down a date and stay with it.

    I will start_____on this date_____

    I will do_____on this date_____

    I contacted_____on this date_____

    I am doing_____as of this date_____

Fitzgerald (1994, pp. 249-250) shares some thoughts of when you know you're getting better. Some of the following ideas are adapted from *The Mourning Handbook*:

How you know when you're getting better...

    ❧ When you can recall both pleasant and unpleasant memories

    ❧ When you can drive somewhere by yourself without crying the entire time

    ❧ When you begin to look forward to the holidays

    ❧ When you reach out to help someone else in need

    ❧ When time passes and you haven't thought about your loved one

    ❧ When you can sit through your church service without crying

    ❧ When you develop your own daily life routine

    ❧ When you no longer make daily or weekly trips to the cemetery

   ℞ When you begin to laugh again

   ℞ When you no longer feel tired all of the time

   ℞ When you wake up in the morning and enjoy seeing a new day

   ℞ When you can take time to enjoy the beauty around you

As you begin and continue to walk through your new single life and you have to make your own decisions, you have to dine alone, you have to walk through the mall alone, you have to travel alone, you have to do just about everything alone—remember that as you move through each day you are becoming a new person.

You are in essence creating your new identity in each day that dawns—you are moving from widowhood or widowerhood to a new selfhood. You'll be making decisions about where you want to establish your life and what kind of work you want to give your life to. Although the circumstances that brought you to this point are tragic, you have the unique opportunity to turn your tragedy into triumph, become a new person, and create a whole new life.

The journey of grief is yours and yours alone. The development of your new life will take time. Pace yourself and don't expect things to happen overnight, but take small steps daily and you will reach your goals and eventually become a new you. Simply be yourself and know that it's all right to focus on you for a while.

Be good to yourself, treat yourself, become comfortable with who you are. You have a destiny to fulfill in your life and only you can allow it to unfold.

Chapter Ten

Nutrition, Exercise, and Grief

Hope is the anchor of the soul,
the stimulus to action, and the
incentive to achievement

– Anonymous

Grief affects the entire person, not just the emotions, and is physically demanding. The body's natural response to grief is often a weakening of the immune system. Physically, you may feel fatigued all of the time or lethargic and feel as though you don't have the energy to do anything. Emotional grief work takes a lot of physical energy. Wolfelt (2001) says that good self-care is often the aspect many grievers tend to ignore. Individual grievers will experience different physical reactions to grief. Some individuals may experience a loss of appetite, some an increase in appetite as a result of the stress grief causes.

It is important to keep a healthy balanced diet and try to keep some form of exercise in your daily or weekly routine. Below are some suggestions and tips for nutrition and exercise to help you stay physically strong as your body expends its energy in emotional grief work.

The Rest Factor:

Allow yourself to rest. Your body is spending a lot of energy grieving and you will feel more fatigued than normal. You may come home after a long day and fall asleep, but be wide awake again just a few hours later. Sleep is an important part of your body healing itself; if you are unable to sleep, go to your physician for something to help you sleep for a short period of time just to break the cycle. If you are able, allow yourself to take power naps, which are 15–20-minute naps during the day. Try not to nap too close to bedtime because you don't want to interrupt your sleep cycle in the evening.

The following strategies are adapted from Fitzgerald (1994, pp. 244-245), *The Mourning Handbook*:

- Set a routine; go to bed at the same time and awaken at the same time.
- Drink warm milk before bedtime because it has a natural sedative.
- Exercise; try to find the time of day that is best for you to incorporate an exercise routine. Some people rest better when they exercise in the evenings. Some find it better to exercise in the morning.
- Try not to watch TV in bed; read a good book or listen to relaxing music right before bedtime.
- Make sure the temperature in your room is comfortably cool, not warm or hot.
- Perform your meditation or prayer routines before bedtime.
- Avoid caffeine or alcohol before bedtime.

Your nutrition is a vital part of your normal health functioning, but when you are grieving, it is even more important to keep a healthy balanced diet. Some individuals when they experience the stress of grief lose their appetite, some have an increased appetite, and most of us just don't pay attention to eating healthy during our time of grieving. See a certified nutritionist and stay on a healthy diet. When we eat junk food or too much sugar we can experience times of "crashing" during the day. Your goal is to keep your blood sugar at a normal level and keep from having food-related "crashes" during the day. Again, this is a time to invest in yourself and take care of yourself. If you've never paid attention to your diet before, now is a good time to start.

A good way to make sure that you are eating a healthy diet is by organizing your eating each day. Bob Greene (2002) in his book *Get With the Program* suggests organizing your meals in the following categories:

- Eating a healthy breakfast
- Eating a moderate lunch
- Snacking in between only if you are hungry
- Eating a moderate dinner
- Stopping eating at least two hours before bedtime

Greene also suggests ways to identify if you're eating due to emotions versus true hunger. The seven most common reasons that people eat due to emotions are:

1. Boredom
2. Stress
3. Loneliness
4. Emotional turmoil
5. Filling a void
6. Anger
7. Fatigue

Most if not all of these areas are related to and experienced during the grief process. Keep a journal of what you eat daily. If you find that you are eating out of boredom, ask yourself "What do I want to do?" and find an alternate activity that you can do instead of eating.

If you are eating out of stress, take some time during each day to log what you are eating, when you are eating, and note if you are eating after a stressful event:

Monday:

- Breakfast: _____
- Lunch: _____
- Dinner: _____
- Snack: _____
- Did you eat anything outside of these times? If so, did you eat after a stressful event? _____

Tuesday:

- Breakfast: _____

- Lunch: _____

- Dinner: _____

- Snack: _____

- Did you eat anything outside of these times? If so, did you eat after a stressful event? _____

Wednesday:

- Breakfast: _____

- Lunch: _____

- Dinner: _____

- Snack: _____

- Did you eat anything outside of these times? If so, did you eat after a stressful event? _____

Thursday:

- Breakfast: _____

- Lunch: _____

- Dinner: _____

- Snack: _____

- Did you eat anything outside of these times? If so, did you eat after a stressful event? _____

Friday:

- Breakfast: _____

- Lunch: _____

- Dinner: _____

- Snack: _____

- Did you eat anything outside of these times? If so, did you eat after a stressful event? _____

Saturday:

- ❧ Breakfast: _____
- ❧ Lunch: _____
- ❧ Dinner: _____
- ❧ Snack: _____
- ❧ Did you eat anything outside of these times? If so, did you eat after a stressful event? _____

Sunday:

- ❧ Breakfast: _____
- ❧ Lunch: _____
- ❧ Dinner: _____
- ❧ Snack: _____
- ❧ Did you eat anything outside of these times? If so, did you eat after a stressful event? _____

Eating due to loneliness is a very easy bad habit to fall into particularly if you are a widow or widower. It's easy to grab comfort food on your Friday or Saturday nights and watch TV on the couch. If you find yourself on the couch more and more on the weekends, call your friends and go out with them. Do something to get yourself out of the house and to stay healthy in your social life.

You can also eat due to the emotion of depression. If you are eating due to depression, contact your physician and get your depression under control. Exercise can help with depression as well.

Take a moment to reflect upon your eating patterns. Write down if you are eating only when you are hungry or if you are eating for another reason. Each time you eat, ask yourself, "Why am I eating?" "Am I truly hungry?"

_____

_____

_____

_____

_____

Richardson, MA, RD, and co-owner of The Fitness Clinic in Los Gatos, California, shares some nutrition strategies to help during the grieving process. Grief is a form of stress that, if prolonged, can damage the body by:

- Accelerating atherosclerotic plaques
- Increasing the likelihood of high blood pressure
- Increasing abdominal obesity
- Increasing insulin resistance and Type 2 Diabetes
- Decreasing the immune response, making you more susceptible to disease.

Sometimes people who are grieving a loss are still responsible for other aspects of life such as children, parents, or business concerns. It is important to maintain the healthiest possible lifestyle during the grieving process. Consider what the airline industry tells people, "Put on your own oxygen mask, and then assist others." It is vitally important for you to be "oxygenated" in order to get through the grieving process without inflicting damage on yourself or others.

Nutritionally, there are several strategies to maintain balanced brain chemistry, which will help decrease stress:

- Maintain adequate nutrition and hydration—eating may be the last thing on your mind, but you must maintain energy (mental and physical) in order to get through the grief process.
- Choose smaller more frequent meals rather than a few large meals for sustained energy throughout the day.
- Balance protein, fat and carbohydrates as each component has a special function with respect to balancing brain chemistry and alleviating stress.
- Minimize caffeine (less than 200 mg/day), alcohol (one drink or fewer per day), and stimulants.
- Include plenty of fresh fruits and vegetables.
- Make sure your diet includes Omega 3 sources such as cold water fatty fish, nuts, nut butters, blueberries, or mango.

Karl Malmsheimer, MA, fitness trainer, and co-owner of The Fitness Clinic in Los Gatos, California, shares a brief workout that you can incorporate into your daily routine, in the morning or when you get home from work.

Physical exercise is very important in your grief recovery journey as well. Exercise releases the natural chemical endorphins in your body that can help regulate your emotions, decrease stress hormones, decrease depression, and improve sleeping patterns. You should incorporate some form of physical exercise into your daily routine, but you don't have to be a hard core athlete to experience the physiological changes in your body.

Walking is one of the easiest and most convenient ways to incorporate movement into your daily routines. It does not require a gym membership and you can start right outside your front door. Walk in the sunlight so that your body stimulates the manufacture of Vitamin D as well as increases the serotonin levels in the brain.

Another option is to have simple 15–20-minute routines that you can do at home without any equipment. Make sure you are cleared for physical activity by your physician and that you modify any exercises to your ability level. The important thing to do is MOVE!

Physical exercise routine:

1. Warm up with 30–60 seconds of marching in place alternating with some low-impact jumping jacks.

2. With a secure chair or bench, do 10–15 seat touches alternating with 10–15 pushups (pushups can be done against a wall or from a chair).

3. Repeat 1 and 2.

4. Do 30–60 seconds of a side-to-side step alternating with a torso twist where your elbow touches the opposite knee.

5. Using a chair as a balance point if needed, do a static lunge 10–15 times on each leg alternating with bicep curls (standing or sitting) using a weighted object.

6. Repeat 4 and 5.

7. Repeat 1.

8. Holding a weighted object in one hand, lean over a chair and pull the elbow up 10–15 times. Repeat for the other arm. Alternate this one arm row with 10–15 chair dips.

9. Repeat 1 and 8.

10. Finish with some core work and stretches such as crunches, pelvic tilts, twists, and bends.

This routine will give you some ideas for basic movements needing no equipment. More advanced routines can be customized using gym equipment, so ask your fitness professional for help.

Chapter Eleven

Returning to Work and Grief

The road to happiness lies in two simple principles:
Find what it is that interests you and
that you can do well, and when you find it,
put your whole soul into it—every bit of energy and ambition
and natural ability you have.

– John D. Rockefeller III

Many individuals who are grieving the loss of a loved one have to return to work after their bereavement leave. Most organizations provide a 3-day leave, some provide a 5-day bereavement leave. Regardless if you have had 3 days, 5 days, or even more, you are going back to work while you are still grieving. Going back to work will add stress to the already stressful time of grief that you are experiencing.

As you go back to work remember that because of your emotional state of grieving, you may not be able to think as clearly as you did prior to your loss. Your productivity may be reduced and you may experience mental and physical fatigue more quickly during the day. When you go back to the workplace remember that you are experiencing something different in your life than the rest of your colleagues and many might not understand what you are going through. Here are some suggestions that you can do to help reintegrate back into the workplace as you continue your grieving process.

Steps for Returning to the Workplace

☐ Contact your manager, if you haven't already, and tell him or her about your loss.

☐ Ask your manager, if possible, to adjust your productivity expectations for a few weeks.

☐ If possible, try to work partial days during the week or a flexible schedule.

☐ Be aware of your emotional and mental state daily.

☐ Try to get fresh air at lunch time and breaks—sunlight and fresh air will help boost your mood during the day.

☐ Contact your organization's Employee Assistance Program counseling resources or take time during the week to meet with your grief counselor.

☐ Work with your manager so if you feel as though you are getting emotional, you can take a break somewhere private.

Activity:

What is your current job title?

_____

Write down any specific areas of your job that you might have difficulty performing initially:

_____

_____

_____

_____

_____

Strategies to assure accuracy and timely completion of work:

- Review your work a second time.
- Reread any written work an hour or more after you have completed a document. This will give you a fresh perspective.
- Have a second person briefly review your work.
- Take time to leave the workplace and go out to lunch.
- Break up your large projects into small tasks.
- Write down "to do" lists to help you remember things that need to be completed.

Activity:

Managing emotional triggers at work by identifying if anything at work triggers your emotions:

Does any part of your job trigger anger?

_____

_____

_____

_____

_____

Does any part of your job trigger tears?

_____

_____

_____

_____

_____

Are there any other job responsibilities that trigger different emotions at work?

_____

_____

_____

_____

_____

Talk with your manager to put strategies into place to help you manage your emotions in the workplace.

_____

_____

_____

_____

_____

Activity:

Identify if anything in your workplace could potentially cause exacerbation of your grief.

Remember that any type of change in the workplace can impact your grief response. If you're dealing with layoffs, workplace re-organization, large scope change, new processes or initiatives, it will increase your stress level and potentially cause an increased grief response within you.

Write down anything that is happening within your workplace that is impacting you or potentially could trigger the grief response within you:

1. _____

2. _____

3. _____

4. _____

5. _____

Workplace Activity:

Schedule a consistent 15–20-minute meeting with your manager once a week, then once every two weeks, then once a month, until you get to the place where you believe you are fully integrated back into normal functioning at your job.

Use the following calendar to schedule your appointments and write down the conversations you had with your manager. Write what you learned from your meeting times.

Calendar Month: _____

Sunday	Monday	Tuesday	Wednesday	Thursday	Friday	Saturday

Appointment and Discussion Worksheet

My manager is: _____

I will schedule or have scheduled my first 15-minute appointment on:

_____

I will talk to my manager about:

_____

_____

_____

_____

_____

What I learned from my meetings with my manager is:

_____

_____

_____

_____

_____

Strategies that I learned to use in the workplace that are most helpful for me in performing my job are:

_____

_____

_____

_____

_____

Strategies for managers in the workplace to help the grieving employee

Steps for helping grieving employees:

1. Listen to your grieving employee and respond to him or her with empathy and receptive body language such as head nods, eye contact, and verbal affirmations.

2. Let your employee know that it is okay to share his or her story at the proper times. You can show interest by saying, "Do you want to share more?" "How do you feel now?" "Are you okay here at work?" "Is there anything I can do for you now?"

3. Show your understanding by rephrasing what your employee has said. For example, "I hear you saying that…" "It sounds like you're feeling…"

Jeffreys (2005) shares some strategies for supporting grieving employees in the workplace:

- Put any of your own loss aside and focus on the employee's loss.
- Be okay with being silent and just listening.
- Let the employee know that it's okay to express his or her feelings.
- Honor the employee's confidentiality.
- Honor your commitments. If you say let's have lunch or coffee and talk, then follow through with your offer.
- Allow enough time to talk with your grieving employee such as break times.
- Plan a regular time to meet with your grieving employee so that you can keep communication open and consistent.
- Let colleagues know it's okay to talk to the bereaved employee.
- Encourage colleagues to attend the funeral or memorial services.
- Give colleagues educational information on grief.

Life, laughter, and love are worth pursuing;
Life transforms us
Laughter fills us
Love carries us

— Dr. Carolyn M. De Leon

Chapter Twelve

Your New Day—Beyond Grief

If one advances confidently in the direction of his dreams,
and endeavors to live the life which he had imagined,
he will meet with success unexpected in common hours.
— Henry David Thoreau

Yes, there is life beyond grief! This section should be used once you've come through the initial months and 1–2 years of grief. Remember that your timeframe for grieving will be different from anyone else's. You may feel as though you've come through your grief in 1 year or you may take 3–4 years to completely move through the process. Each person is unique—you are unique.

As sure as the sun rises every day, you will have a new day rise in your life—one that will be without the pain and emotions of grief. Just as Spring follows Winter, you will have a new Spring in your life. Your life will be different because you will have changed as a result of your grief and the loss of your loved one.

Last and First Steps:

Take responsibility for your life: You now have to take full responsibility for your life. You are not responsible for your loved one any longer. It's time to put away any responsibility that you have tied yourself to with your loved one who is now gone. Jack Canfield (2005) in his book *The Success Principles* writes that you have to take 100% responsibility for your life and give up any excuses for not moving forward in your new life.

Change your thinking: By this time, you must change your thinking. Change your negative thought patterns to positive thought patterns. Instead of thinking and saying "I can't because…"; "It won't happen because…"; "I can't do that…"; change your words to, "I can do all things…"; "I see this happening"; "All things are possible"; "I will do…." It's a matter of changing your perspective from a half-empty glass to a half-full mentality.

Do something new: Let yourself come out of your box. Learn something new, visit new places, let yourself come outside the box of old ways. If you think you don't like live theatre, try it again! If you think you don't like museums, try them again! You must discover a whole new you. And as we grow in life, our likes and dislikes change. Try going fishing, try walking on the beach, try reading a book under the shade in a hammock. Try new restaurants and new ethnic foods, travel to places you've never been to before.

Two New Personal Goals

Write down two goals that you can accomplish—one within one year and the other within two years:

I can accomplish_____by_____

Steps to accomplishing your goal:

_____

_____

_____

_____

_____

I can accomplish_____by_____

Steps to accomplishing your goal:

_____

_____

_____

_____

_____

Gratitude Journal

Every day in the morning or in the evening take some time in solitude and write down what you are grateful and thankful for in your life. Verbalize aloud daily.

_____

_____

_____

_____

_____

_____

_____

_____

_____

_____

_____

_____

_____

_____

_____

_____

_____

_____

_____

Envision your new life: Take some time to reflect upon what you want your life to be and where you would like it to go.

Visualize a new life—write down what it looks like to you:

_____

_____

_____

_____

_____

Write the goals that you want to reach in your new life:

_____

_____

_____

_____

_____

Write down steps that you will take to reach your goals:

_____

_____

_____

_____

_____

_____

_____

_____

_____

_____

You have learned a lot about yourself during your journey through grief. Take some time and reflect on how you have noticeably changed:

_____

_____

_____

_____

_____

_____

_____

_____

_____

_____

From what you have learned throughout your journey, how can you now help someone else who is in need or traveling through the same journey?

_____

_____

_____

_____

_____

_____

_____

_____

_____

Chapter Thirteen

Internet Organizational Resources

I shall not pass this way again:
Then let me now relieve some pain,
Remove some barrier from the road,
or brighten some one's heavy load.

— Eva Rose Park

    American Association of Suicidology

http://www.suicidology.org

    American Cancer Society

http://www.cancer.org/docroot/home/index.asp

    American Foundation for Suicide Prevention

http://www.afsp.org

    Friends for Survival Inc.—California suicide survivor network

http://www.friendsforsurvival.org

    American Hospice Foundation

http://www.americanhospice.org

    Mothers Against Drunk Driving (MADD)

http://www.madd.org/

    National Hospice Palliative Care Organization (NHPCO)

http://www.nhpco.org

    National Organization for People of Color Against Suicide (NOPCAS)

http://nopcas.com/

    National Sudden Infant Death Syndrome

www.sids.org

- National Suicide Crisis Hotline Numbers

  http://suicidehotlines.com/

- Parents of Murdered Children (POMC)

  http://www.pomc.com

- Parents without Partners—Single Parents Support

  http://www.parentswithoutpartners.org/

- SAVE (Suicide Awareness/Voices of Education)

  http://www.save.org

- SIEC (Suicide Information & Education Collection)

  http://www.suicideinfo.ca/

- SPANUSA (Suicide Prevention Action Network USA, Inc)

  http://www.spanusa.org

- The Center for Grief and Loss for Children

  http://www.griefcenterforchildren.org/

- The Compassionate Friends—Grief support after the loss of a child

  http://www.compassionatefriends.org

- Yellow Ribbon Suicide Prevention Program

  http://www.yellowribbon.org/

Visit www.dawningofanewday.org

Order the companion book *Dawning of New Day: A Journey Out of Darkness; Life Lessons to Help You Through Grief*

Go to Inkwaterbooks.com or Amazon.com to order your copy today

E-mail the author at: drcarolyn@dawningofanewday.org

References

Agel, J., & Glanze, W. D. (1987). *Pearls of wisdom: A harvest of quotations from all ages.* New York: Harper Collins.

Canfield, J. (2005). *The success principles: how to get from where you are to where you want to be.* New York: Harper Collins.

Colgrove, M., Bloomfield, H. H., & McWilliams, P. (1991). *How to survive the loss of a love.* Los Angeles: Prelude Press.

Davidson, J. D., & Doka, K. J. (Eds.). (1999). *Living with grief at work, at school, at worship.* Washington, D.C.: Hospice Foundation of America.

Deger, S., & Gibson, L. A. (Eds.). (1993). *The book of positive quotations* (2nd ed.). Minneapolis: Fairview Press.

Deits, B. (2004). *Life after loss.* Cambridge, MA: Life Long Books.

DeLeon, C. M. (2008). *Dawning of a new day; A journey out of darkness* (2nd ed.). Portland: Inkwater Press.

Doka, K. J., & Davidson, J. D. (Eds.). (1998). *Living with grief: who we are, how we grieve.* Philadelphia: Brunner/Mazel.

Fitzgerald, H. (1994). *The mourning handbook.* New York: Fireside.

Fitzgerald, H. (2000). *Grief at work: A manual of policies and procedures.* Washington, D.C.: American Hospice Foundation.

Ginsburg, G. D. (1995). *Widow to widow.* Cambridge, MA: Da Capo Press.

Greene, B. (2002). *Get with the program.* New York: Simon & Schuster.

Grollman, E. A. (1977). *Living when a loved one has died.* Boston: Beacon Press.

Hewett, J. (1980). *After suicide.* Philadelphia: Westminster Press.

James, J. W., & Friedman, R. (1998). *The grief recovery handbook.* New York: Harper Collins.

Jeffreys, J. S. (2005). *Coping with workplace grief.* Boston: Course Technology.

Kübler-Ross, E. (1974). *Questions and answers on death and dying.* New York: Collier Books.

Kübler-Ross, E., & Kessler, D. (2005). *On grief and grieving.* New York: Scribner.

Lawrenz, M., & Green, D. (1995a). *Life after grief: How to survive loss and trauma.* Grand Rapids, MI: Baker Books.

Lawrenz, M., & Green, D. (1995b). *Overcoming grief and trauma.* Grand Rapids: Baker Books.

Noel, B., & Blair, P. D. (2003). *I wasn't ready to say goodbye.* Fredonia, WI: Champion Press.

Pink, M., & Pink, B. (1995). *Grace for grief.* Grand Rapids: Word Publishing.

Pinkney, M. (2002). *Pocket positives for living.* Victoria, Australia: The Five Mile Press.

Williams, M. B., & Poijula, S. (2002). *The PTSD workbook.* Oakland, CA: New Harbinger Publications.

Wolfelt, A. D. (2001). *Healing your grieving heart: 100 practical ideas.* Fort Collins, CO: Companion Press.

CPSIA information can be obtained at www.ICGtesting.com
Printed in the USA
LVOW02s1730051113

360110LV00006B/759/P